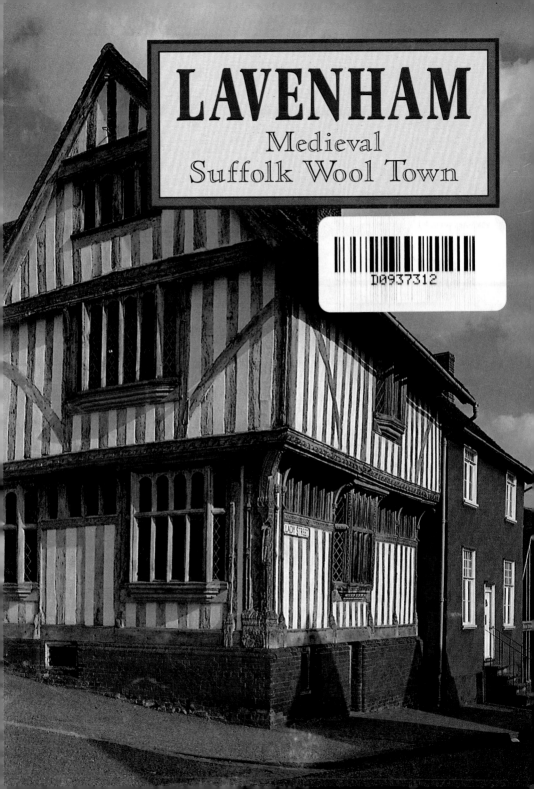

LAVENHAM

Medieval
Suffolk Wool Town

Little Hall

Lavenham and its Story

Situated in the south-west corner of Suffolk, surrounded by undulating countryside, Lavenham stands proudly on the top of a hill, with the smaller weaving villages nestling in the Brett Valley.

Acknowledged to be one of the finest examples of a medieval wool town, most of the timbered houses in Lavenham were built between 1450 and 1500: whole streets of timbered houses, not just

1

the odd one here and there. That is what makes Lavenham unique.

A Wars of the Roses town, a country village and an artist's delight, Lavenham is all of these and more. There is something to see at the turn of every corner. Words are not enough to show how shops and guildhalls, pubs and weavers' houses, manor house and hunting lodge, rich merchants' houses and farmhouses jostle and crowd each other as they step down the steep streets; nor to tell of the joy of a farm within sight of the Market Place or of the fields which stretch up and out over the eastern horizon. Preservation orders on most of the houses, individually and in blocks where the frontages warrant it, should preserve Lavenham for posterity. Trees have been 'preserved' too and in 1967 overhead wires were placed underground in the main streets, restoring much of the former beauty of the village scene.

Lavenham began to assume its present shape in the thirteenth century. A market place was formed on the top of the hill and houses built by the sides of the tracks leading down from it. The track between the two manor houses of Overhall and Netherhall became the HIGH STREET. Here the distorted and leaning frame of the CROOKED HOUSE is evidence of the strength and adaptability of the medieval oak timbers.

Already a centre of an area producing and exporting wool, cloth weaving assumed greater importance when Flemish weavers settled in England in 1334. Some came to Lavenham and built their houses in WATER STREET. This street takes its name from the stream which flows down its entire length. This was culverted at an early date, probably in the 15th century and served dye houses along its length.

By 1381 Lavenham's trade was growing and although a large band of men from the village joined the mob under John Wrawe of Sudbury, the Peasants Revolt in that year scarcely made itself felt. Lavenham was far too busy to notice!

By 1425 the SWAN INN, the White Horse, the Crown and Anchor and houses such as Nos. 6–7 Market Place were in being and a master weaver, Thomas Spring I had set up his looms and founded a family fortune. His eldest son, Thomas II, became a very wealthy Clothier. The Swan was already venerable in 1544 when John Newton left it in his will to Robert Cooke shoemaker and Elizabeth his wife; it was built in 1400.

The Wars of the Roses did not affect the increasing prosperity of

2

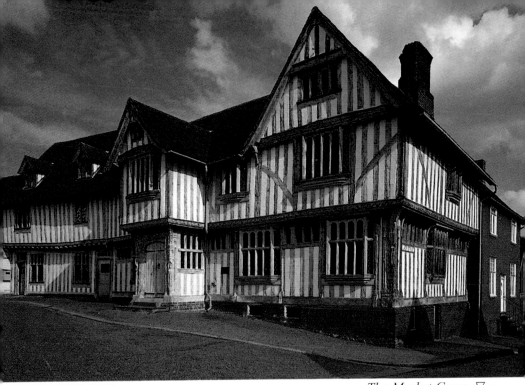

△ *The Guildhall*

The Market Cross ▽

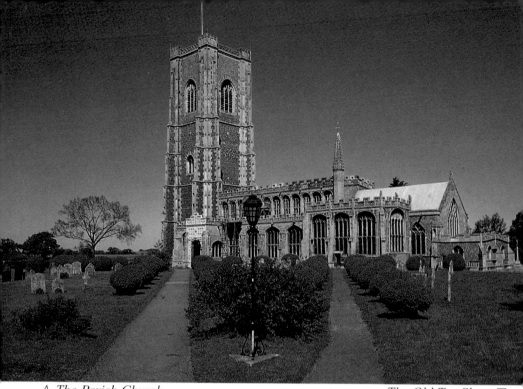

△ *The Parish Church*

The Old Tea Shop ▽

the place either. There was an enormous demand for the blue serge cloth for which Lavenham was renowned throughout Europe and workers flooded into the area. The resulting pressure for houses produced the Lavenham of to-day.

Every sort of building, of every shape and size, was squeezed into any available space. Merchants living in houses hitherto quite good enough for family and goods, either built bigger and better ones in more desirable spots or expanded their premises as best they may, even to putting a new roof over the existing one, tiles and all, to 'keep up with the neighbours'. Increasing contact with the Continent resulted in the desire for more gracious living so that Lavenham became in many respects a model new town. Prentice Street, Bolton Street, and Shilling Street all take their names from the Clothiers who built their big houses there. John Shilling's house is known as SHILLING GRANGE and was built at the end of the fifteenth century. Isaac Taylor, the engraver, rented the house in 1786 for £6 a year. His daughters Ann and Jane are well known for their poems, particularly Jane's 'Twinkle, twinkle little star'.

In 1485 the Lord of the Manor, John de Vere, 13th Earl of Oxford, led the vanguard of Henry VII's victorious army at the Battle of Bosworth and returned to find Lavenham a large and flourishing place. As a thank-offering for his safe return, Earl and Merchant, Thomas Spring II, united to give Lavenham her greatest glory, the PARISH CHURCH, one of the finest parish churches in England. Dedicated to Saint Peter and Saint Paul it is 191½ feet long and 68 feet wide. The Nave is 43 feet high and the Tower, sentinel of the countryside, 141 feet high with the Spring coat-of-arms round the top 32 times and the Star of the de Veres set in the flintwork half way down.

The architecture is entirely Perpendicular except for the Chancel which is of the Decorated period. The interior has cathedral-like proportions with graceful arcades and rich carving. A restoration in the last century removed several lovely features like the hammer-beam roof in the chancel, and the rood-screen gates which, happily, were recovered – rumour says – from the use of penning a churchwarden's pigs!

There is a Parclose in each of the side aisles but except for these, and one mural monument and three brasses, the church is singularly uncluttered with memorials. Emblems of the Oxfords and Springs abound, particularly the de Vere Star and the Spring

"Cordwainers"

Merchant Mark on the shields at the base of the Tower. The peal of eight bells is world famous; the tenor bell was made by Miles Graye of Colchester in 1623.

A pleasant walk down to the village goes through the meadow called Saffron Paynes, at the back of the Church, reached by the path at the east end. The Earl lived to see the greater part of the Church completed, but it was Thomas Spring III, the rich Clothier, who left sufficient money in 1523 to finish the Tower and the South Chapel, build the richly carved Parclose in the North Aisle and endow it as a Chantry. Opposite the church is the OLD TEA SHOP, a typical thatched Suffolk cottage and a rarity among the red tiles of prosperous Tudor Lavenham.

The wool trade reached its peak during Thomas III's lifetime and tales of his outstanding wealth reached the ever eager ears of Henry VIII, so Thomas paid his taxes twice. In 1524 Lavenham was the fourteenth wealthiest town in England, exceeding much larger places such as York, Lincoln and Gloucester.

Other Clothiers such as Simon Braunche, to whose memory the South Aisle Parclose was erected, William Causton, Robert Groome and William Rysby gave generous support to the building of the Church.

William Causton's woolhall, now known as LITTLE HALL, dates mainly from the 14th and 15th centuries and stands just off the Market Place behind the Market Cross; it is now the headquarters of the Suffolk Preservation Society. The slender stone pre-Reformation Cross is the focal point of the MARKET PLACE. It was erected in 1501 with money left by a merchant, William Jacob. The market toll-keeper's cottage stands on an island site behind the cross. A weekly market was held in the Market Place until the mid-18th century, and there were four fairs a year. These have all been abolished.

Three Guilds were formed in the town to regulate the cloth trade and THE GUILDHALL, which was the hall of the Guild of Corpus Christi, still survives. Built in the 1520s on the south side of the Market Place it became the centre of the cloth-making industry after the religious side of the guild was suppressed. The Merchant Clothiers met there to govern every aspect of the trade. Over later centuries it has been successively Town Hall, a Prison, the county Bridewell and House of correction, a workhouse and a wool store.

In 1555 the Reverend Rowland Taylor was confined in the

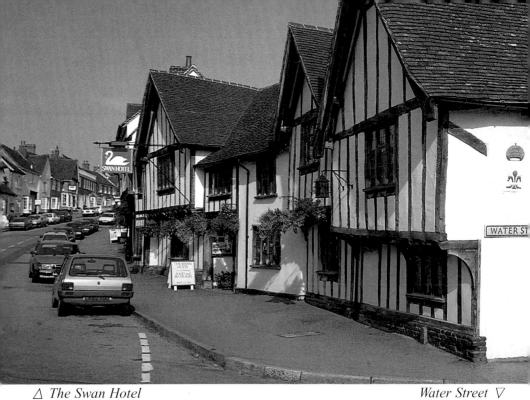

△ *The Swan Hotel*　　　　　　　　　　　　　　*Water Street* ▽

△ *The Wool Hall*

Little Hall ▽

Guildhall for two days before going to the stake at Aldham, near Hadleigh. In 1950 Sir Cuthbert Quilter gave the whole group of buildings to the people of Lavenham for whom the National Trust administers the property.

One other guild hall remains. Known as THE WOOL HALL, it was built in 1464 by the religious guild of the Blessed Virgin on the corner of the street which takes its name from the guild – Lady Street. This is a typical building of the period, having a central floor-to-roof hall with a king-post roof and a two-sided gable on either side. After the suppression of the religious guilds, the hall was used for the buying and selling of woven cloth and spun yarn and was divided into three houses when the spinning industry went into decline.

The building was almost entirely demolished in 1911 but was restored after strong protests were made against removal. In 1963 it was bought by Trust Houses Ltd. and incorporated into the Swan Hotel. St. Peter's Guildhall in the High Street was demolished in 1896 and Holy Trinity's hall in Prentice Street in 1876.

In 1578 Queen Elizabeth visited Lavenham, escorted by the High Sheriff of Suffolk, Sir William Spring, grandson of the rich Clothier. The whole court accompanied her, amongst whom was the Lord of the Manor Edward de Vere, 17th Earl of Oxford, reputed by some to be the author of Shakespeare's plays.

Towards the end of the 16th century many of the merchants and clothiers left Lavenham when the cloth industry declined. Later the spinning of fine wool yarns increased and Lavenham became famous again. It was a common sight to see the women sitting outside their cottages in the streets, spinning wool for markets in London, Norwich and Ireland.

A Grammar School was opened in Barn Street in 1647. Among its scholars were John Constable the landscape painter, Arthur Young, who became famous as a writer on agriculture and William Clubbe, the poet, born at Whatfield near Hadleigh in 1745.

About 1750 a drastic change was made in the appearance of many of the overhanging timbered houses when the bottom portion was brought flush with the top part. The fronts were then rebuilt with bricks in the style of the Georgian period.

For nearly 150 years little happened in Lavenham. Trade dwindled and poverty was rife, but with the opening of a branch railway line from Long Melford to Bury St. Edmunds, a steam flour mill was built in 1865 and three years later, the first beet-sugar factory; this latter enterprise was not a success. There was a renewal of the weaving industry towards the end of the 19th century with the manufacture of horse hair cloth for seating, but change in fashion after the Great War killed it and the looms fell silent again. The railway closed in 1965, the flour mill in 1968.

A wall plaque on the site of the old British School is dedicated to the 487th U.S.A. Bomb Group which was stationed at Lavenham Air Base during the 1939–45 war. The Memorial to the men of Lavenham who gave their lives in two wars is in the Parish Church.

To-day new housing estates and a playing field have extended Lavenham beyond the western medieval boundaries and, with some good, some more controversial, infilling and with the introduction of some light industries, the population has risen to above 1400 once again after the long years of stagnation and decline.

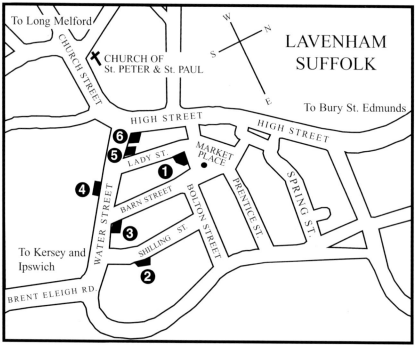

1. THE GUILDHALL   2. SHILLING GRANGE   3. FLEMISH WEAVERS COTTAGES
4. de VERE HOUSE   5. WOOL HALL   6. THE SWAN HOTEL

Printed and published by J Salmon Ltd.,
100 London Road, Sevenoaks, Kent TN13 1BB
Copyright © 1997 J Salmon Ltd.
ISBN 1 898435 69 3

*Time has touched me gently in his race,
and left no odious furrows in my face.*

George Crabbe

ISBN 1-898435-69-3

9 781898 435693

A SALMON CAMERACOLOUR® BOOK